CENGAGE Learning

Novels for Students, Volume 16

Project Editor: David Galens

Editorial: Anne Marie Hacht, Sara Constantakis, Ira Mark Milne, Pam Revitzer, Kathy Sauer, Timothy J. Sisler, Jennifer Smith, Daniel Toronto, Carol Ullmann Research: Sarah Genik

Permissions: Debra Freitas, Shalice Shah-Caldwell

Manufacturing: Stacy Melson

Imaging and Multimedia: Lezlie Light, Kelly A. Quin, Luke Rademacher Product Design: Pamela A. E. Galbreath, Michael Logusz © 2002 by Gale. Gale is an imprint of The Gale group, Inc., a division of Cengage Learning Inc.

For more information, contact
The Gale Group, Inc.
27500 Drake Rd.

of the editors or publisher. Errors brought to the attention of the publisher and verified to the satisfaction of the publisher will be corrected in future editions.

ISBN 0-7876-4899-X
ISSN 1094-3552

Printed in the United States of America
10 9 8 7 6 5 4 3 2 1

A Gathering of Old Men

Ernest J. Gaines 1983

Introduction

A Gathering of Old Men (1983) by Ernest J. Gaines is a novel about race relations in the American South. The action takes place over the course of one day in rural Louisiana. A white man has been shot dead and lies in the yard of a black man's house. Eighteen old black men gather at the house and each claims that he is responsible for the killing. The brutal white sheriff conducts his investigation as the old men await the revenge of the dead man's relatives, who have a fearsome, longstanding reputation for exacting vigilante justice against black people. By the end of the day, there have been many surprises, and many of the characters have changed in ways that they could not have imagined. The conclusion of the novel hints that although the wounds of the past run deep and still influence the present, times are changing, and in the future, black people can hold out hope for a new era in which everyone is treated equally under the law.

A Gathering of Old Men was Gaines's fifth novel. Gaines is an African American who was born and raised on a plantation in Louisiana, a fictional version of which is the setting for all of his work. His novels and short stories have been widely acclaimed for the accuracy with which he captures the language of rural African Americans in Louisiana, and the way he envisions the possibility of positive change for his characters, even those who are caught in the most difficult of circumstances.

Author Biography

Ernest J. Gaines was born on January 15, 1933, on the River Lake Plantation near New Roads, Pointe Coupee Parish, Louisiana. He was the son of Manuel (a laborer) and Adrienne J. (Colar) Gaines. As a boy, Gaines worked in the plantation fields near Baton Rouge, Louisiana. In 1948 he moved to Vallejo, California with his mother and stepfather, (Gaines's parents separated when he was young). Gaines read voraciously in the Vallejo Public Library but found nothing that resonated with his own experience of life, since all the writers he read were white and did not portray blacks accurately.

Gaines attended Vallejo Junior College before being conscripted into the army in 1953. He served until 1955, writing fiction during his off-duty hours. After military service he enrolled at San Francisco State College (now University), where he majored in English. His short story, "The Turtles," which appeared in the magazine, *Transfer*, was his first published work. Gaines graduated with a Bachelor of Arts degree in 1957 and was awarded the Wallace Stegner Creative Writing Fellowship, which enabled him to pursue graduate study in creative writing at Stanford University from 1958 to 1959.

Gaines continued to publish short stories, one of which, "Comeback," won the Joseph Henry Jackson Award from the San Francisco Foundation in 1959. His first novel, *Catherine Carmier*, set on a plantation in rural Louisiana, was published in 1964. A second novel, *Of Love and Dust*, with a similar setting, followed in 1967.

A collection of stories, *Bloodline*, appeared in 1968 and one of those stories, "A Long Day in November," was published separately as a children's story in 1971. In 1971 Gaines was a writer in residence at Denison University, Granville, Ohio, and it was during this year that his most well-known and widely acclaimed novel, *The Autobiography of Miss Jane Pittman*, was published. In 1972 the novel received an award from the Black Academy of Arts and Letters, and the fiction gold medal from Commonwealth Club of California. It was made into a television movie in 1974.

Gaines's fourth novel, *In My Father's House*, was published in 1978 followed by *A Gathering of Old Men* in 1983. The latter was made into a television movie in 1987.

More recognition came Gaines's way in 1987, when he received a literary award from the American Academy and Institute of Arts and Letters. He had already received honorary doctorates of letters from Denison University (1980), Brown University, (1985), Bard College (1985), and Louisiana State University (1987).

In 1983 Gaines became professor of English and writer in residence at the University of Southwestern Louisiana, Lafayette, Louisiana.

Gaines's 1993 novel is *A Lesson before Dying*,

which won a National Book Critics Circle Award for Fiction in 1993 and was nominated for a Pulitzer Prize.

Plot Summary

The first narrator in *A Gathering of Old Men* is a black boy, Snookum. He says that Candy has instructed him to run and tell some of the local people to gather at Mathu's house. Snookum sees Beau lying in the yard, and Mathu tells him to go away. Snookum runs off on his errand.

At Marshall House, Jack Marshall is asleep and drunk on the porch, and his wife Bea is in the pasture. When Snookum arrives with his message, Janey, the housekeeper, calls Lou Dimes and Miss Merle. When Miss Merle arrives, Janey tells her there has been a killing. Miss Merle drives to Mathu's house where a group of men has gathered, some of them with shotguns. Candy tells her that she killed Beau, but Miss Merle does not believe her. Candy says that Mathu claims to have shot Beau and that two of the other old men also claim to have shot him. Candy asks her to get more people there with twelve-gauge shotguns and empty number five shells, so they can all claim they committed the killing.

Chimley is fishing with his friend Mat when they get the message to go to Mathu's house. They are scared because they know the whites will seek revenge for the killing of Beau. But they feel they ought to go to Mathu's since he was the only one they knew who had ever stood up to the whites. They agree to get a ride with Clatoo.

Mat waits for Clatoo to arrive and argues with his wife Ella. He tells her not to try to stop him from going to Marshall. Clatoo arrives with Billy Washington, Jacob Aguillard, Chimley, and Cherry Bello. As they head for Mathu's house with guns, they are scared but determined. They pick up Yank and Dirty Red. As they near Mathu's house, Clatoo lets them off and goes back for more men. They walk together and reach a graveyard, where each man visits his family plot. Clatoo returns with more men.

There are now eighteen old men at Mathu's house. Mathu says that when the sheriff arrives he will turn himself in, but all the other men claim that they are the killers. Reverend Jameson pleads with Mathu to turn himself in and tells the others to go home, but no one listens to him.

Lou Dimes arrives from Baton Rouge. Candy again claims that she killed Beau, but Lou knows she is lying. He tells her that Fix, Beau's father, will come looking for blood. Mapes arrives and he does not believe Candy either. He slaps Billy Washington and Gable, but both men still insist that they killed Beau. Then Mapes hits Reverend Jameson. Mapes believes that Mathu is the killer, but he cannot persuade anyone to change his story. Billy Washington says he did it because thirty years earlier, Fix's men had beaten his son. But Mapes knows that Billy cannot shoot a gun accurately.

Mapes questions Mathu, who admits his guilt but refuses to tell the other men to go home. Ding Lejeune says he killed Beau because of what the whites did to his sister's young daughter. Johnny Paul claims he did it to preserve the memory of his family who worked the fields with plows and mules before the tractors came. Tucker explains how all the best land has been given to the Cajuns, and how Felix Boutan beat his brother Silas to death. Yank recalls how he used to break all the horses, but has had nothing to do since the tractors came. Gable tells how forty years ago, his sixteen-year-old son was sent to the electric chair for raping a white girl on questionable evidence. Coot, a veteran of World War I, tells of injustices against black servicemen.

Gil Boutan gets the news that his brother has been killed. It is the day before a big football game between Louisiana State and Mississippi. Sully drives him to where the old men are gathered, but Mapes tells Gil to go home. Miss Merle brings food and they all eat. She is bewildered by the strange situation in the house.

Sully drives Gil to his home where family and friends are gathered. Gil tells his father Fix that Mapes does not want him to go to Marshall until he is sent for. Luke Will and some of the others want to go there immediately and lynch Mathu. But Gil pleads with his father not to, because his own chances of making All-American at LSU will be shattered if he is involved in anything illegal. Gil's brother Claude says he will do whatever his father says, but another brother, Jean, agrees with Gil. Fix reacts bitterly and banishes Gil and Jean from his house. He tells the others there will be no lynch mob, although Luke Will does not accept his decision.

The narrative moves to Tee Jack's store, where there are several customers, including Jack Marshall and a quiet man who teaches at the University of Southwest Louisiana. Jack is uninterested in making conversation. Luke Will and his friends enter, and Luke hints at what they plan to do. When the teacher tries to persuade them not to, they force him to leave.

Back at the house, Mapes announces that Fix will not be coming, but at first the men do not believe him. Then Mathu says he will turn himself in, but Clatoo asks Mapes for a few minutes in which they can talk. Candy protests at being excluded, and Mathu tells her to go home. Lou hauls her off and throws her in the back of her own car. Mapes gives them fifteen minutes to talk. Clatoo says there is no one to fight and they should go home. The others protest and say they will go to jail with Mathu. Mathu says it is the proudest day of his life because he has finally seen the men stand up for themselves. He tells them to go home too, but then Charlie steps forward, saying Mathu does not have to go anywhere.

Lou and Candy return and hear that Charlie has confessed. He says that Beau attacked him with a stalk of sugar cane, and Charlie hit back. He ran to Mathu's house, and Mathu told him not to run from Beau, and gave him his own gun. Beau came into the yard, loading his gun, and Charlie shot him. Then Charlie ran away, asking Mathu to take the blame. But just before sunset he realized he must return. Mapes and Charlie step out onto the porch, only to hear Luke Will demanding that Charlie be handed over.

Mapes is wounded by a shot by Luke Will, and all the men except Jean Pierre and Billy Washington stream out of the house. They break up into three groups. There are several exchanges of gunfire, and one of the lynch mob is injured. Snookum tries to get out of harm's way. Outside, under the house, he sees that Mapes is unable to get up. Mapes tells Lou that he, Lou, is in charge.

Leroy Hall, the wounded man, snivels and pleads to give himself up. Luke Will kicks him and tells him to shut up. Luke asks Mapes to stop the blacks from shooting and he will turn himself in, but Charlie is in charge and refuses the offer. He heads for the tractor, which shelters Luke Will. There is more shooting, and Charlie and Luke Will are both killed.

For the trial that takes place later, the courthouse is packed, and half of those in attendance are from the news media. All the defendants, black and white, are put on probation for five years, and banned from possessing guns or being with anyone who has them.

Characters

Jacob Aguillard

Jacob is one of the old black men. His sister Tessie was killed by white men in 1947. He carries his gun like a soldier, and he takes part in the final shootout.

Robert Louis Stevenson Banks

See Chimley

Cherry Bello

Cherry Bello is a seventy-four year old black man who owns a liquor and grocery store. He is one of the men who gathers at Mathu's house.

Grant Bello

See Cherry Bello

Charlie Biggs

Charlie Biggs is a big, fifty-year-old black man. All his life he has been timid and submissive, but he finally learns to stand up for himself when he kills his employer, the abusive Beau, who is going to shoot Charlie. After the killing, Charlie hides for a while but finally realizes he must come back to face up to the consequences. He believes that by his actions he has finally become a man, and he insists on being called Mr. Biggs. He is killed in the shootout with the lynch mob.

Myrtle Bouchard

See Miss Merle

Beau Boutan

Beau is the aggressive, racist Cajun farmer who leases the plantation from the Marshall family. Beau attacks Charlie, who shoots him dead. He is mourned only by his own family.

Claude Boutan

Claude Boutan is one of Gil's older brothers. He drives a truck for an oil company. In the meeting at Fix's home, he says he will do whatever Fix decides.

Media Adaptations

- An audio tape titled *A Gathering of Old Men/ Readings* was produced in 1987 by Amer Audio Prose Library.

- Volker Schlöndorff directed a made-for-television adaptation of *A Gathering of Old Men* (1987).

Fix Boutan

Fix Boutan is the father of Beau. For many years he and his family and other like-minded whites have been able to take the law into their own hands. They have a long history of beating, killing, and abusing black people. As everyone expects, Fix wants to go to Marshall to lynch the killer of Beau. But two of his sons, Gil and Jean, oppose him, and Fix calls the lynching off. He says that the family must act as one, and if they disagree, he will not act. Fix says that he never wants to see his sons Gil and Jean again, but at the end of the novel there is a hint of reconciliation between Fix and Gil, as they sit together in the courtroom.

Gil Boutan

Gil is a student at Louisiana State University and he is an outstanding football player, the best fullback in the Southern Conference. Known as Salt because he plays so well with Cal, who is called Pepper, Gil desperately wants to be an All-American, like Cal. Unlike the rest of his family, he is not a racist, and after the killing of Beau he urges his father not to take the law into his own hands. He is bitterly upset when his father banishes him from the house.

Jean Boutan

Jean Boutan is one of Gil's older brothers. He is in his mid-thirties and owns a butcher's shop in Bayonne. Like Gil, he tries to persuade Fix not to send a lynch mob to Marshall, saying that they should allow the legal process to take care of the situation.

Sidney Brooks

See Coot

Matthew Lincoln Brown

See Mat

Cal

See Calvin Harrison

Candy

Candy is the strong-minded, independent, thirty-year-old niece of Jack and Beatrice Marshall. Her parents were killed in an automobile accident when she was five, and she was mostly raised by Miss Merle and Mathu. Her boyfriend is Lou Dimes. Candy is small and thin, with close-cropped hair. She wants to protect Mathu, and she insists that it was she who killed Beau. It is also her idea to summon the men to bring shotguns and empty number five shells, so that they can all claim to have killed Beau. When Mapes arrives, Candy is vigorous in her defense of the black men, and contemptuous of Mapes. Later, she becomes resentful when all the men want to discuss the situation in private. Mathu tells her to go home, and Lou bundles her into the back seat of her own car. In the courtroom scene at the end of the novel, Mathu asserts his independence from her, while she and Lou are reconciled.

Chimley

Chimley is a seventy-two-year-old black man

who is fishing with his lifelong friend Mat when he is summoned to Mathu's house. His first reaction is fear, remembering how the white people react after any violent incident, but he puts this aside and decides to go. Before he leaves he tells his wife to make sure his food is ready for him when he returns.

Antoine Christophe

See Dirty Red

Clatoo

Clatoo is one of the leaders of the black men. He drives many of them to Mathu's house in his truck, and he tells them to carry themselves like soldiers. He hates Fix because Fix's brother Forest tried to rape one of his sisters just before World War II. Like the other black men, Clatoo claims to have shot Beau. It is Clatoo who organizes the scheme whereby the men reload their shotguns, and it is he who stands up to Candy, telling her that the men are going to have a meeting without her. During the shootout, it is Clatoo who organizes the black men.

Coot

Coot goes to Mathu's house proudly wearing his World War I uniform. He says that when he got home from the war, a white man told him never to wear his uniform again, since people in that part of the world did not like black men wearing medals for killing whites. But the day of Beau's killing, Coot decided to wear his uniform and shoot anyone who laughed at him or told him to take it off. He claims he shot Beau when the Cajun would not stop coming toward him with his gun.

Lou Dimes

Lou Dimes is a white man who has been seeing Candy for three years. He works as a journalist for a newspaper in Baton Rouge, and appears not to share the racist attitudes of most of the white characters. He arrives at Mathu's house when Janey calls him and says that Candy needs him. Lou takes little part in the action himself but he closely observes and reports on what happens. In the shootout, the injured Mapes puts Lou in charge of the situation, and Lou unsuccessfully tries to negotiate a truce between Luke Will and Charlie.

Louis Alfred Dimoulin

See Lou Dimes

Dirty Red

Dirty Red, one of the old black men, always has a self-rolled cigarette hanging from the side of his mouth. He is the last of his family, and he has a reputation for laziness. But he acquits himself well in the shootout.

George Eliot Jr.

See Snookum

Griffin

Griffin is Mapes's young deputy. He is a slender, unimpressive man, ready to bully the defenseless but wary of anyone he thinks might fight back. Just before the shootout begins, he tells Mapes that he will not use his gun against white men in defense of black men.

Leroy Hall

Leroy Hall is a boy of seventeen who associates with Luke Will and his friends. He is wounded in the shootout and whines like a coward.

Calvin Harrison

Calvin, known as Cal, is a black football player who plays alongside Gil so well that the two of them are known as Salt and Pepper. Cal has been nominated for All-American.

Glo Hebert

Glo Hebert is the grandmother of Snookum, Toddy. and Minnie.

Herman

Herman is the coroner who collects Beau's body. He is in his mid-sixties.

Albert Jackson

See Rooster

Beulah Jackson

Beulah Jackson is Rooster's wife. She says she is ready to go to jail with the men.

Reverend Jameson

Reverend Jameson is the only black man who does not have a gun, and he is despised by the other men. He is short and bald, with a white mustache and beard. He is scared of what may happen and pleads with the men to go home, but no one listens to him. But even Reverend Jackson refuses to give Mapes the answers he wants, even when Mapes hits him.

Janey

Janey is the housekeeper at the Marshalls' house. She is scared when Snookum tells her about the killing, and repeatedly calls on Jesus to help her. Miss Merle bullies her into making a list of people who do not like Fix.

Bing Lejeune

Bing Lejeune is a mulatto who is one of the men at Mathu's house.

Ding Lejeune

Ding Lejeune is Bing's brother. He has a grudge against Fix because he believes his sister's child was poisoned by one of the Cajuns.

Mapes

Mapes is the white sheriff. He is in his late sixties, about six feet three, and heavy. He is a bully and starts his investigation by hitting three black men in quick succession. With the exception of Mathu, he does not respect the blacks. However, Mapes does try to avoid more bloodshed by instructing one of his men to keep Fix away from the house, and trying to persuade Mathu, whom he believes is guilty, to turn himself in. He also learns to respect Charlie Biggs. Mapes is slightly wounded in the final shootout, and has to sit on the porch, unable to get up. In the courtroom scene, he is embarrassed by having to admit his inability to do anything to stop or resolve the shootout.

Beatrice Marshall

Beatrice Marshall is Jack's wife. She shows no interest when she hears that Beau has been killed, since she has never liked him.

Jack Marshall

Jack Marshall owns the plantation but takes no interest in it, passing his responsibilities on to his niece, Candy. He drinks every day in Tee Jack's store, and seems to have no interest in anything in life. He knows that the situation at Mathu's house is dangerous but he refuses to do anything to defuse it.

Mat

Mat is seventy-two-years old; his closest friend is Chimley. He and Chimley decide that for once in their lives they are going to stand up for themselves against the whites. Mat refuses to tell his wife where he is going, and they quarrel. He weeps with anger over injustices that his family has suffered but he is determined finally to do something with his life.

Mathu

Mathu is a black man in his eighties. He is tall and dark-skinned, and is proud of having no white blood. His ancestors came from Senegal in Africa. Mathu is the only one of the blacks who all his life has stood up for himself, not letting the whites push him around. He once beat Fix in a long fistfight. This is why Mapes is so ready to believe that Mathu killed Beau, since Mapes does not think any of the other blacks would have been capable of it. Mathu helped to raise Candy, and that is why she tries to protect him, but he is willing to take the blame for the killing of Beau, even though he did not do it.

Miss Merle

Miss Merle is a family friend of the Marshalls. She helped to raise Candy and has known her for over twenty-five years. Janey thinks she is good-natured, but Miss Merle has a patronizing attitude toward the black men. When she takes sandwiches to the people in Mathu's house, she expresses anger to Candy and Mapes, and is bewildered by the strange situation.

Johnny Paul

Johnny Paul is one of the first of the old men to say he shot Beau. He reminisces about the past, when the blacks worked in the fields with hoes and plows from dawn to sunset, before the days of the tractor. He says he killed Beau to stop the tractors plowing up the graveyard and erasing all memory of his own people.

Pepper

See Calvin Harrison

Gable Raund

Gable Raund is one of the black men who claims he shot Beau, and he refuses to change his story even when Mapes hits him. He is angry because over forty years ago his sixteen-year-old son was sent to the electric chair after being unfairly convicted of raping a white girl.

Cyril Robillard

See Clatoo

Janice Robinson

See Janey

Rooster

Rooster is married to Beulah Jackson. Clatoo describes him as "yellow, with nappy black hair."

Rufe

Rufe is one of the first of the black men to arrive at Mathu's house and one of the first to claim that he shot Beau.

Russell

Russell is the deputy charged by Mapes to stop Fix coming to Marshall.

Salt

See Gil Boutan

Joseph Seaberry

See Rufe

Sharp

Sharp is one of the whites who accompanies Luke Will in the lynch mob. Like Luke Will, he is a truck driver.

Snookum

Snookum is the young boy who is sent by Candy to tell the neighbors to assemble at Mathu's house. He lives with his grandmother, Glo Hebert, and has a sister, Minnie, and a brother, Toddy.

Thomas Vincent Sullivan

See Sully

Sully

Sully is a friend of Gil and Cal. Like them, he is a football player, although a mediocre one. His main hobby is watching television. It is Sully who drives Gil to his father's house.

Tee Jack

Tee Jack owns a grocery and liquor store. He is a racist and does not care who knows it. He is intimidated by Luke Will and his friends when they come into the store, and he has to be careful of what he says in case they cause trouble.

Jacques Thibeaux

See Tee Jack

Horace Thompson

See Sharp

Cedric Tucker

Cedric Tucker is a quiet black man who usually keeps himself to himself. At Mathu's house, he tells the story of his brother Silas, who was the last black sharecropper at Marshall. Silas was killed by the whites in a fight after he had dared to perform better with his two mules than Felix Boutan did on his tractor.

Billy Washington

Billy Washington is one of the old black men. He is a terrible shot, and could not hit the side of a barn. The others tease him about it. Mapes hits him but he continues to insist that he shot Beau. He says it was because Fix and his men beat his son so hard his brain was permanently damaged.

Luke Will

Luke Will is a truck driver and a friend of Beau. He is big and rough looking, and is a racist who leads the lynch mob to Marshall. He is killed in the shootout.

Yank

Yank is one of the black men who go to Mathu's house. He is in his early seventies, and he used to break in the horses. He resents the whites because their tractors rendered horses unnecessary.

Themes

Racism

Racism pervades the novel, which shows that blacks have suffered discrimination and abuse for many generations. The racism continues even into the late 1970s. Many of the whites, including Luke Will and Tee Jack, routinely use the offensive word "nigger" to describe any black person. The Cajun Boutan family are guilty of innumerable ugly incidents involving blacks. The law either looks the other way or accepts a skewed version of events, as is revealed, for example, in the incident related by Tucker, in which his brother Silas was beaten to death by whites because he had dared to perform better with his mules than they did with their modern tractors. Tucker says, "Where was the law? Law said he cut in on the tractor, and he was the one who started the fight." In the story related by Gable, the word of a white girl of dubious reputation is enough to unjustly send a black boy of sixteen to the electric chair.

Sheriff Mapes's attitude when he first arrives at Mathu's house is testimony to the way whites treat blacks. When he does not get the answer he wants, Mapes resorts to beating three of the old men. That is the only way he knows how to deal with black people. When that does not work, he does not know what else to do.

As well as suffering abuse as individuals, blacks are also collectively discriminated against. When the white landowning Marshall family leased the land to sharecroppers (tenant farmers), they gave the best land to the Cajuns who had never been on the land before, and the worst land to the blacks even though the blacks had been working the land for a hundred years. This ensured the continuing poverty of the blacks.

Topics for Further Study

- Have race relations improved in the United Have race relations improved in the United States since the 1970s? What are some of the problems associated with race relations and how can they be addressed in a constructive manner?

- Gaines is sometimes accused of creating negative stereotypes in his portrayal of white people. Is there any truth in this in *A Gathering of Old Men*? How are the whites such as Mapes, Fix Boutan, Gil Boutan, and Luke Will presented?

- What role do the black women play in the novel? Do they share in the empowering of the black men? What kind of relationship do black men such as Chimley and Mat have with their wives?

- Choose a character from the novel and write a narration of the trial scene from that person's point of view.

There is also a hint that racism exists amongst the blacks as well. Mathu, who is very dark-skinned, prides himself on the fact that he has no white blood in him, and he looks down on others who have mixed blood, like Clatoo, who had a white grandfather and an Indian and black grandmother, and Rooster, who according to Clatoo is "yellow, with nappy black hair."

There are signs, however, that things are changing. Not only does the Boutan family decide not to seek vigilante justice as they did in the old days (even though family friends like Luke Will do not respect the decision), but Mapes develops a respect for a black man, Charlie Biggs, that he never had before. Finally, the close partnership between

Cal and Gil, a black man and a white man, on the football field is a parable of how things might and should be between the two races. As Sully explains, they are of equal ability, and they work hard for each other:

> Wherever you went, people spoke of Salt and Pepper of LSU. Both were good powerful runners, and excellent blockers. Gil blocked for Cal on sweeps around end, and Cal returned the favor when Gil went up the middle.

Attaining Manhood

When the old black men decide to stand up for themselves after a lifetime in which they have passively endured humiliation and abuse, they finally become men in their own eyes. They face up to a challenge with courage instead of running from it or hiding.

Alone amongst the black men, Mathu has always managed to do this. He has always retained his dignity as a man and stood up to the whites. This has involved him in many fights, including one that Chimley recalls—a toe-to-toe fight between Mathu and Fix that broke out after Mathu refused Fix's request to return a bottle to the store. This is why Mathu is respected by Mapes, who regards him as a real man. It also explains why Mapes is so ready to believe that Mathu killed Beau, since Mapes does not think that any of the others would have had the courage to do it. Mapes does not regard the others as real men.

The theme of attaining manhood begins early in the novel, in the first sections narrated by black men. Chimley and Mat agree that this time it would take more strength to crawl under the bed than it would to stand up to Fix and his men. Mat says he has to go to Mathu's house because this may be his last chance to do something with his life. It must be remembered that the old black men are voluntarily walking into a highly dangerous situation in which they fully expect a lynch mob to appear at any minute to avenge a killing that each one of them is going to claim he committed. But they feel good and are determined to be courageous. As they approach Mathu's house, for example, "Jean Pierre, Billy Washington, and Chimley was doing all they could to walk with their heads up and backs straight."

When the men are interrogated by Mapes, they seem to get stronger every minute. They do not look down at their feet in a submissive posture but are able to look Mapes straight in the eye. They also talk back and mock him, to his bewilderment. They also mock Griffin, the young deputy, who, it is implied, has a long way to go before he attains real manhood. Griffin is ready to talk big and bully the defenseless but he has no real strength or authority. No one respects him, not even his boss, Mapes. And when Mapes tells him to stop Candy from blocking the door, Griffin backs off when he sees she is ready to punch him.

The theme of manhood becomes fully explicit in the character of Charlie. Charlie is the most timid of the black men. No one even considers that he might have been the killer. Although he has been bullied for years by Beau, he has never answered back or stood up for himself. Nevertheless, when Beau is ready to kill him, he finds the courage to defend himself. But Charlie's growth is not yet complete, because his first action is to run away and leave Mathu to take the blame. However, after hiding for a few hours, Charlie realizes what he has to do, and after he confesses to the crime he repeatedly exclaims his newfound self-respect:

> "I'm a man, Sheriff," Charlie said. "I want the world to know I'm a man. I'm a man, Miss Candy. I'm a man, Mr. Lou. I want you to write in your paper I'm a man."

Charlie's self-respect is also apparent in his request to be called Mr. Biggs. Mapes, who now has some respect for Charlie, is happy to oblige. From that point until Charlie's death, he is the man in charge of the situation, not Mapes, or Lou Dimes, and certainly not the would-be lyncher, Luke Will. When Charlie dies, leading a charge on the enemy, it is the death of a man, not a boy.

Structure and Point of View

The novel is divided into twenty short chapters or segments, each of which is narrated in the first person. There are fifteen different narrators, ten black and five white (this is fewer than the number of chapters because Lou Dimes narrates four chapters, and Snookum and Sully two each). Dimes is given four chapters probably because Gaines thought him well suited, as a journalist, to report on events. Dimes supplies much objective information, since he adopts a fairly neutral stance, favoring neither the old men nor Mapes. The segments are also arranged with pacing and emotional tension in mind. Gaines stated in an interview that he tried to arrange the narratives of the different black men for variety. He wanted to avoid having two highly emotional segments following in succession.

Gaines's original idea was to have the novel narrated entirely by Lou Dimes, but he decided that this method was unsatisfactory because it could not capture the language that he wanted. The multiple narrative that he finally decided upon captures a variety of voices. Each narrator supplies not only his or her own point of view on the action but also an individual voice. The voice of Janey, for example, as she constantly appeals to Jesus for divine aid, is very different from that of the boy

Snookum, who rushes off on his errand "spanking my butt the way you spank your horse when you want him to run fast." The language that Mat and Chimley use as they narrate their segments about fishing together is also very distinctive, with its use of black dialect that deviates from standard American English. It is quite different from the objective narrative of Lou Dimes, told in standard English, whose voice is in turn distinguished from the other white characters such as Tee Jack, Sharp, and Sully. In the long reminiscences and stories of the black characters in the segment narrated by Rufe, Gaines has also captured something of the quality of the oral tradition of storytelling that is a part of black culture in the region.

None of the major characters, such as Mapes, Candy, Mathu, Luke Will, Gil, Charlie, or Fix, is allocated a narrative segment. This means that these characters are revealed solely through what they say and do and what others say about them. The reader is given no direct insight into their thoughts (even though sometimes the narrators do offer comments on what Mapes is thinking, but that is still their opinion, formed from their perspective, not that of Mapes).

Gaines said he could not have Candy or Mathu narrate because they know too much about what happened, and this would have spoiled the effect for the reader. Mathu, for example, could hardly have avoided hinting that he did not kill Beau, but for the sake of telling a good story, Gaines wants this to come as a surprise to the reader. Saving this revelation for the end also helps to establish in the reader's mind the central idea that Charlie's act was not his alone. The accumulation of all the stories of racial injustice told by the other black men make it clear that everyone, black and white, is involved in the shared history of a single, albeit divided, community, and that everyone bears some responsibility for what finally happens.

Lynching in the South

The long list of injustices suffered by the old blacks in the novel, including the threat and the reality of lynching, is rooted in the real experience of black people in the South. According to Stewart E. Tolnay and E. M. Beck, in *A Festival of Violence: An Analysis of Southern Lynchings, 1882–1930*, there were 2,805 documented lynchings between 1882 and 1930 in ten southern states. Approximately 90 percent of the victims were African Americans. This means that on average, one black person was lynched by a white mob every single week from between 1882 until 1930, although in reality the lynchings reached a peak in the 1890s and declined afterwards. Victims were often tortured and mutilated before their deaths, and parts of their bodies were sold as souvenirs.

The four states with the worst records were Mississippi (463 lynchings, 1882–1930), Georgia (423), Louisiana (283) and Alabama (262). In Louisiana six lynchings occurred in Pointe Coupee Parish, where Gaines was born and raised, between 1881 and 1908. Some of these were "private" lynchings, carried out by relatives and friends of the victim; others were by a posse (groups of men appointed by the sheriff to track down suspects) or by a mass group. The last lynching in Louisiana, of a black man accused of intent to rape, occurred in 1946. The year 1951 was the first year since records began in 1882 when there were no lynchings anywhere in the south. The last officially recorded lynching in the United States occurred in 1968.

The fictional old men in the novel (which is set in 1979) were born sometime between the last years of the 1890s and the first decade of the twentieth century, making them well able to remember what happened to black people during this period. In the novel, Fix and his confederates are known and feared for their lynchings. In real life Louisiana in the 1920s and 1930s, eighteen men were lynched, fifteen of whom were black, including two men who were lynched on the same day in 1928, their only offense apparently being that they were the brothers of a murderer.

Tolnay and Beck list seventy-five reasons given for lynching black men. These included, in addition to murder, robbery, and rape: acting suspiciously, gambling, quarreling, adultery, acting "improper" with a white woman, arguing with a white man, indolence, inflammatory language, being disreputable, being obnoxious, insulting a white man or woman (a black man named George Paul was lynched in Pointe Coupee Parish in 1894 for offending a white man), courting a white woman, demanding respect, trying to vote, voting for the wrong party, and unpopularity.

Some of these killings took place before the victim's arrest and some afterwards, often with the connivance of the authorities. Even if the black person accused of a capital offense was given a trial, the legal system was stacked against him. Although he would be given a lawyer, the lawyer was often inexperienced and given neither the time nor the resources to mount an effective defense. The verdict was often preordained, and was followed by swift execution.

Compare & Contrast

- **1930s:** The southern United States is a largely segregated society. Blacks face institutionalized discrimination in all aspects of their work and social life. They are excluded from positions of power and treated as second class citizens. Many are denied the right to vote.

  1960s: As the Civil Rights movement gathers momentum and affirmative action programs are introduced by private and public employers, a new era in race relations begins. However, there is a long way to go before the legacy of hundreds of years of injustice can be completely removed.

  Today: In terms of racial justice, southern states are almost unrecognizable from what they were fifty years ago. Alabama and Mississippi, for example, are now the two states with the highest number of African Americans elected to government offices. However, racism has not been eradicated, and problems in race relations remain.

- **1930s:** Capital punishment reaches a peak in the United States, with an average of 167 executions per year.

  1970s: In 1972, the Supreme Court declares the death penalty unconstitutional, but it is reinstated in 1976.

  Today: Many experts regard the death penalty as unfair because it affects black people disproportionately, reflecting conscious or unconscious racism in the judicial system. They point to the following statistics: Of the 752 (as of January 16, 2002) people executed in the United States since the death penalty was reinstated in 1976, 35 percent have been black, 7 percent Hispanic, and 56 percent white. Of those executed for interracial murder, only eleven were whites who killed blacks; 167 were blacks who killed whites. Those who murder whites are more likely to be sentenced to death than those who murder blacks.

- **1930s:** Although on the decline, lynchings still take place in the south. Five lynchings of black men occur in Louisiana.

  1980s: White supremacist groups are on the increase in the United States and incidents of violence against black people and other minorities show a corresponding increase.

  Today: Incidents of racial violence still take place. In 1998 James Byrd, a black man in Jasper, Texas, dies after being chained to a pickup truck and dragged behind it by three whites. Some see this case as a modern-day lynching.

Lynching, as well as other mob violence such as race riots, declined after World War II as the white supremacist group the Ku Klux Klan, which had peaked in membership in the 1920s, went into decline. By the 1950s, the Klan consisted mostly of poorly educated whites (like Luke Will in the novel).

The Civil Rights movement of the 1950s and 1960s ushered in a new era in race relations in the south. It secured voting and other rights for black people and made discrimination illegal. In many parts of the rural south, however, change was slow, as the novel amply demonstrates. Tee Jack's bar, for example, has officially been desegregated for at least fifteen years, but blacks and whites still do not sit in the same place. Blacks buy a drink in the store and drink it outside, since Tee Jack and the white customers find many ways to make them feel unwelcome.

And even in the new era of civil rights, African Americans did not always have the full protection of the law. In an interview given in 1983, Gaines commented that old-style white vigilantism had ended but it was always likely to spring up in new guises. Now, "the Luke Wills are in the police department," he said.

Critical Overview

A Gathering of Old Men was received with unanimous praise by reviewers, who admired Gaines's ability to recreate once again, in his fifth novel, the texture of the lives of black and white people in rural Louisiana, especially the way the people actually spoke.

Reynolds Price, in *The New York Times Book Review*, drew attention to Gaines's "innovative method" of employing so many different first-person narrators, and the unexpected conclusion. He concluded that Gaines had constructed

> with large and single-minded skills, a dignified and calamitous and perhaps finally comic pageant to summarize the history of an enormous, long waste in our past—the mindless, mutual hatred of white and black, which, he implies, may slowly be healing.

Ben Forkner, in *America*, pointed out that the poor conditions under which the blacks live is not entirely due to racism. An underlying theme of the novel "is the simple, natural dispossession of old age, of the traditional and well-loved values of the past, the old trades and the old manners, forced to give way to modern times."

John F. Callahan, in *The New Republic*,

described the novel as "a remarkably original gathering of voices," and praised Gaines's exploration of how the old ways and customs that operate between blacks and whites have changed and continue to do so. He also pointed out that Gaines "does not romanticize anyone, and even the deeply felt and deeply rendered recriminations of the old men are touched with occasional comic posturing, exaggerated emphasis, and obvious preaching."

Mary Helen Washington, in the *Nation*, wrote that the novel's greatest strength lay in its language, which recreated the past:

> These communal voices constitute a kind of collective revision of history, giving proof in their own words of the existence of ordinary people whom the world noticed only briefly in the long-gone era of the civil rights movement.

But Washington was also disturbed by the subordination of women in the novel. Candy, for example, although she is a strong woman, is finally shown as "just another threat to manhood. Women leading men is just another form of slavery, so Candy must be eliminated." Washington noted that black women were silenced also, and this meant that the novel underestimated the contribution made by women in shaping their own history.

The reviewer for *People Weekly* pointed out that although the novel has a serious subject, it "is often very funny." Later critics have examined Gaines's humor in the novel in more detail, as well as other aspects of his language, such as its roots in the oral traditions of southern black culture.

Sources

Callahan, John F., "A Gathering of Old Men," in the *New Republic*, Vol. 189, December 26, 1983, pp. 38-39.

Forkner, Ben, "A Gathering of Old Men," in *America*, June 2, 1984, p. 425.

Price, Reynolds, "A Louisiana Pageant of Calamity," in *New York Times Book Review*, October 20, 1983, p. 15.

Review, in *People Weekly*, Vol. 20, November 14, 1983, pp. 24-25.

Tolnay, Stewart E., and E. M. Beck, *A Festival of Violence: An Analysis of Southern Lynchings, 1882–1930*, University of Illinois Press, 1992.

Washington, Mary Helen, "The House Slavery Built," in the *Nation*, January 14, 1984, pp. 22-24.

Further Reading

Babb, Valerie Melissa, *Ernest Gaines*, Twayne, 1991.

> This text is an analysis of Gaines's work in chronological order, with a chapter devoted to each novel. The emphasis is on Gaines's re-creation in writing of the oral storytelling intrinsic to rural Louisiana.

Estes, David C., *Critical Reflections on the Fiction of Ernest J. Gaines*, University of Georgia Press, 1994.

> This collection contains fourteen essays on all aspects of Gaines's work. On *A Gathering of Old Men*, Sandra G. Shannon writes about Gaines's "defense of the elderly black male," and Milton Rickels and Patricia Rickels discuss folk humor in the novel.

Gaudet, Marcia, and Carl Wooton, *Porch Talk with Ernest Gaines: Conversations on the Writer's Craft*, Louisiana State University Press, 1990.

> This work consists of interviews with Gaines conducted in 1986 and 1987, which explore his development as a writer and the process of transforming folk

narrative and culture into literature.

Papa, Lee, "His Feet on Your Neck": The New Religion in the Works of Ernest J. Gaines," in *African American Review*, Vol. 27, No. 2, Summer 1993, pp. 187-93.

> Gaines's novels focus on religion as a tool for self-definition, and he reinterprets Christianity from the African-American perspective. A number of characters, including Charlie Biggs from *A Gathering of Old Men*, interpret religion in personal terms and undergo an act of martyrdom that helps achieve a communal vision.

Lightning Source UK Ltd.
Milton Keynes UK
UKHW02f1841100718
325517UK00023B/461/P